Miss Mackean

Z099967

First Atlas

Written and designed by

Nicola Wright · Tony Potter · Dee Turner · Christine Wilson

Illustrated by

Lyn Mitchell

Contents

Watts

LONDON • NEW YORK • SYDNEY

All about maps

A map is a picture of a place seen from above. Imagine what your home would look like if you flew over it in an aeroplane and took a photograph. The picture would show the area around your home spread out flat.

This is the view of our home from above. Draw a picture of how you think your home would look.

See how the picture shows the houses, trees and roads.

If you travelled into space you would see other countries as well as your own.

My town

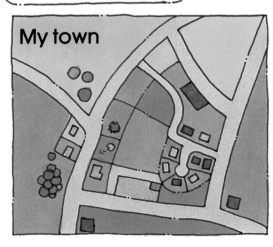

Imagine that you fly higher. Now you can see your whole town or city. Everything looks tiny.

My country

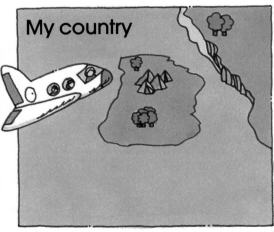

Imagine your town is on an island. As you go even higher you can see the whole island.

The Earth

Clouds form in the sky and swirl around the Earth. There is much more ocean than land.

This is how my country would look as a map. Tiny pictures called symbols are used to stand for real things.

The pictures below are the symbols used in this book. This part of an atlas is called the **key**. The key tells you what the symbols stand for.

If you are looking for a country, go to the list on page 40 and look under the first letter of the country name.
So, **Chile** is under the letter **C**.

Symbols

Symbols

 Country boundaries

 Leafy woodland

 Oceans and Seas *Pacific Ocean*

 Mixed woodland

 Capital cities ■ Moscow

Large cities • Vladivostok

Mediterranean woodland
(dry areas with evergreen trees)

Lakes

Rivers

Desert
(some deserts are just sandy, but some are stony and covered with bushes or cacti)

 High mountains

Low mountains

Grassland
(called **prairie** in North America, and **pampas** in South America)

 Tropical rain forest

Steppe
(scrubland or grassland in Asia)

 Monsoon woodland
(hot areas with a rainy season)

Savannah
(dry grasslands with some trees in Africa)

 Pine forest

Tundra
(frozen land)

Ice

3

World map

This big map shows you what the world would look like if it was flattened out. The differently coloured areas of land are called continents. There are seven continents and four oceans.

This is planet Earth. Imagine a line around its middle. This is called the equator.

This book shows you some of the people, animals, plants and places found in each continent.

The biggest continent is Asia. The smallest continent is Australia.

Countries

The maps in this book show all the countries in the world. A white line shows where one country joins another.

Every country has a flag. Some of them are shown in this book.

The Polish flag

The Belgian flag

The Czechoslovakian flag

The Irish flag

The bottom half of the world is called the southern hemisphere.

Arctic Ocean

North America

Atlantic Ocean

Equator

Pacific Ocean

South America

Atlantic Ocean

South Pole

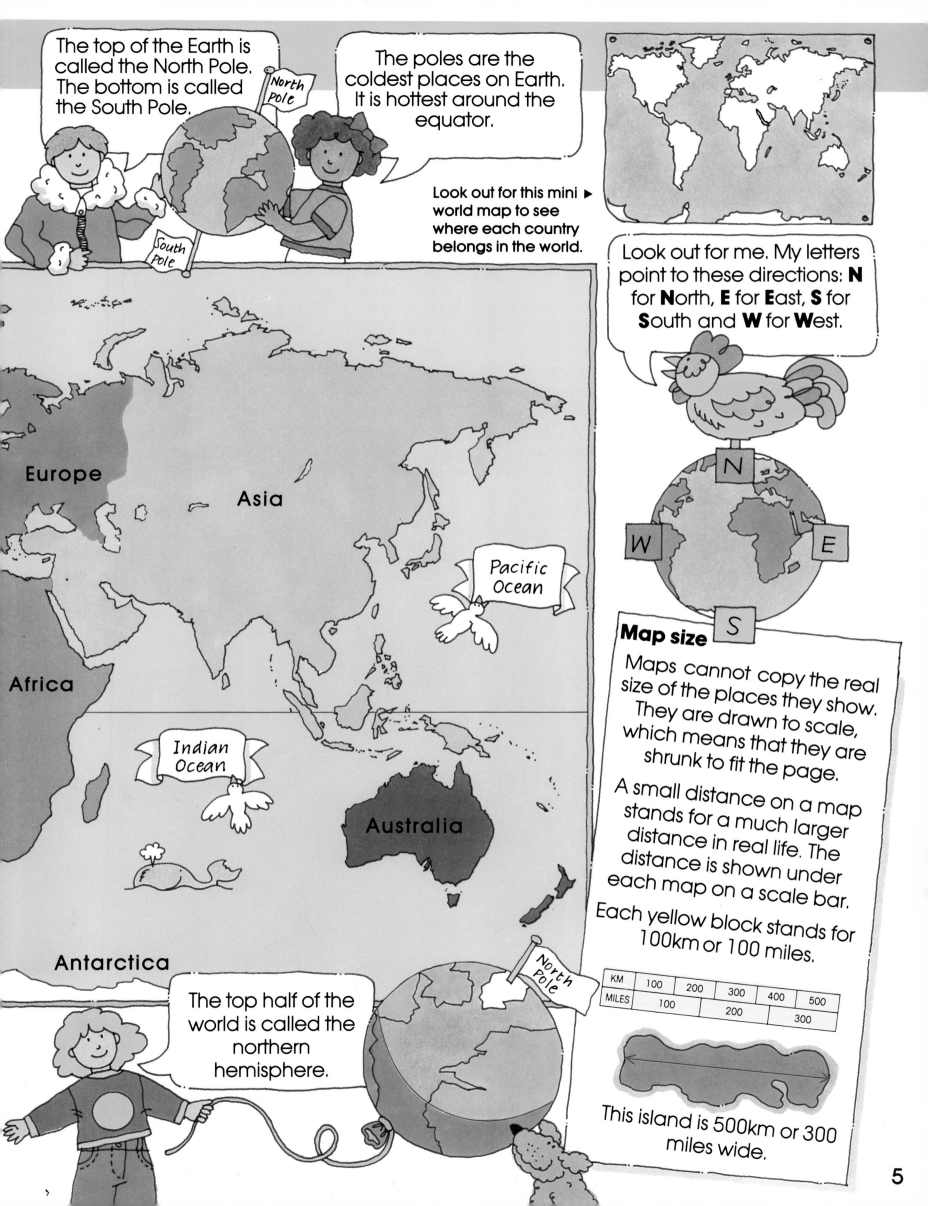

The top of the Earth is called the North Pole. The bottom is called the South Pole.

The poles are the coldest places on Earth. It is hottest around the equator.

Look out for this mini ▶ world map to see where each country belongs in the world.

Look out for me. My letters point to these directions: **N** for **N**orth, **E** for **E**ast, **S** for **S**outh and **W** for **W**est.

Europe

Asia

Pacific Ocean

Africa

Indian Ocean

Australia

Map size

Maps cannot copy the real size of the places they show. They are drawn to scale, which means that they are shrunk to fit the page.

A small distance on a map stands for a much larger distance in real life. The distance is shown under each map on a scale bar.

Each yellow block stands for 100km or 100 miles.

KM	100	200	300	400	500
MILES		100		200		300	

Antarctica

The top half of the world is called the northern hemisphere.

This island is 500km or 300 miles wide.

5

Europe

Europe is the second smallest continent. Only Australia is smaller. It is made up of over 30 countries. Some of them have joined together to form the European Community. Here you can see each country's boundary and capital.

★ = capital city

Reykjavik
Iceland

Iceland is a large island in the North Atlantic Ocean. It is 1,200 kilometres to the west of Norway.

Finland

Sweden

Norway

Helsinki

United Kingdom

Oslo ★

Stockholm

Tallinn
Estonia

Scotland

Edinburgh ★

Northern Ireland

Riga
Latvia

Belfast ★

Lithuania

Republic of Ireland

Copenhagen

Dublin ★

Vilnius
★

Wales

England

Cardiff

Denmark

Russia

Minsk ★

London ★

North Sea

Netherlands

Amsterdam

Berlin ★

Warsaw ★

Belarus

Atlantic Ocean

★ **Brussels**

Belgium

Germany

Poland

Luxembourg

★ **Prague**

★ Paris

Czechoslovakia

Moldova

Liechtenstein

Vienna ★

France

★ **Bern**
Switzerland

Austria

Budapest
★

Kis

Slovenia

Hungary

Romania

★ Ljubljana

Andorra

Monaco

Italy

★ Zagreb

Bucharest ★

Portugal

Croatia

1 Belgrade ★

San Marino

4

Spain

Yugoslavia

Lisbon ★

★ Madrid

3

★ Sofia
Bulgaria

★ Rome

Tiranë 2

Vatican City

Albania

Gibraltar

Greece

Athens

Mediterranean

1 Bosnia & Herzegovina
   ★ Sarajevo

2 Macedonia
   ★ Skopje

3 Montenegro
   ★ Titograd

4 Serbia
   ★ Belgrade

Valletta
Malta

6

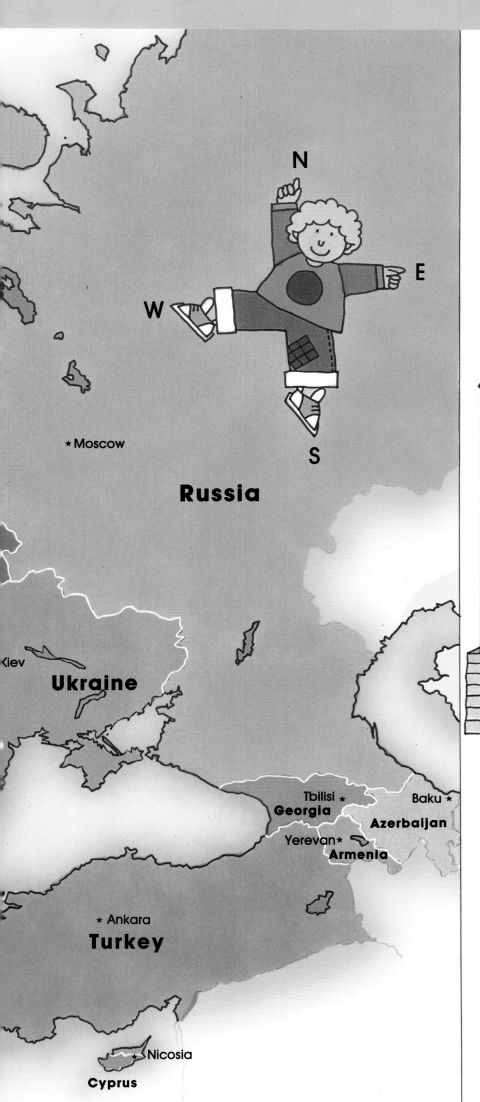

★ Moscow

Russia

Kiev

Ukraine

Tbilisi ★
Georgia

Baku ★

Azerbaijan

Yerevan ★
Armenia

★ Ankara

Turkey

★ Nicosia

Cyprus

European Community

In 1958 Belgium, France, West Germany, Italy, Luxembourg and the Netherlands set up the European Economic Community (now called the European Community or EC).

Since then several more countries have joined the EC, including Denmark, Greece, Republic of Ireland, Portugal, Spain and the United Kingdom. Others are hoping to join.

The EC has its own European Parliament which meets in the French city of Strasbourg.

The EC was set up to make trade between the member countries cheaper and easier.

The EC flag

7

European languages

Here you can see some of the national costumes of several European countries and how people say "hello" in their language.

"Hola" (Spanish)

"Ciao" (Italian)

Traditional costumes are only worn on special occasions like festivals. Most European children wear jeans, sweatshirts and training shoes.

Normally it is difficult for someone from one country to understand what someone from another country is saying because they do not speak the same language.

Spain   Italy

"Ola" (Portuguese)

"Yia sas" (Greek)

Over 30 different languages are spoken in Europe. Some languages, such as Russian and Greek, have a different alphabet.

Portugal   Greece

Weather

The weather in Europe gets warmer as you go further south.

In the mountains it gets very cold in the winter and snow falls.

More rain falls in the west than in the east.

"Bonjour" (French) — France

"Guten Tag" (German) — Germany

"Servus" (Austrian) — Austria

"Dag" (Dutch) — Netherlands

"Shwmai" (Welsh) — Wales

Iceland

"Godan dag" (Icelandic)

"Privyet" (Russian) — Russia

"Zdravo" (Serbo-Croat) — Yugoslavia

"Jo Napot" (Hungarian) — Hungary

"Zdravey" (Bulgarian) — Bulgaria

"Dzien Dobry" (Polish) — Poland

"Hei" (Swedish) — Sweden

In the winter in the far north there are only a few hours of daylight every day.

Many people take their holidays on the Mediterranean coast where the weather is warm and sunny all year.

Countries in the middle of the continent have cold winters, warm summers and plenty of rain.

Produce of Europe

Europe is a big farming area. Many types of crops and animals are farmed.

Many people work in industry in Europe. Factories produce everything from nuts and bolts to computers and aircraft.

There are flat plains in parts of Russia. Large amounts of wheat, oats and barley are grown there.

Mediterranean countries produce fruit, including grapes, olives, oranges and lemons.

Many European countries have coal and iron ore in the ground. Mining it is a big industry.

There are many dairy farms in Britain, France and Denmark. These are cooler countries where lots of rain falls and so the grass grows well. This gives the cows plenty to eat. Cheese and yogurt are made from their milk.

Millions of tourists from all over the world visit Europe every year, providing many jobs.

Wildlife

Chamois look like a mix between a goat and a deer. They live in the mountains of Europe.

Badgers are also found in woodland. They sleep during the day in burrows and feed at night on insects, snails, slugs and small animals.

Foxes live in woods and forests, and sometimes towns. They have beautiful red fur and long, bushy tails.

Hedgehogs are covered with small spines to protect them from attackers. When they are frightened they roll into a tight ball.

Protected golden eagles can be found in the high mountains of Europe.

Barbary Apes are the only monkeys that live in Europe. They are found in Gibraltar, off the southern coast of Spain.

The monk seal has been hunted for years for its fur, oil and meat. Less than 1,000 remain in the Mediterranean Sea.

11

Postcards from Europe

There are many different types of landscape in Europe. There are also many famous places to see. Here are some typical postcard views:

Tulips and windmills in the Netherlands

Brandenburg Gate, Berlin, Germany

Eiffel Tower, Paris, France

Neuschwanstein Castle, Bavaria, Germany

A ski resort in the French Alps

Ponte Vecchio, Florence, Italy

Grand Place, Brussels, Belgium

Farmland in Ireland

Tower of London, London, England

A fjord in Norway

St Basil's Cathedral, Moscow, Russia

The Acropolis, Athens, Greece

Mountains in Austria

Sagrada Familia, Barcelona, Spain

A Greek island

Lapps and their reindeer in Lapland

13

Northern Europe

These northern European countries are known as Scandinavia. Norway has over 150,000 islands along its coastline. The Norwegian coast is jagged, with deep inlets called fjords. Forests and lakes cover large areas of Scandinavia. Many bears and wolves used to live in the forests.

Workers travel to the oil rigs by helicopter.

Children here learn to ski almost as soon as they can walk!

There is oil under the sea bed. Oil rigs are used to pump the oil up to the surface.

The oil is used as fuel for cars and for heating buildings.

Trawlers are fishing boats that catch fish by dragging nets along the sea bed. Many Norwegian fishing boats fish in the North Sea.

Some fishing boats can stay out at sea for months at a time.

Norwegian Sea

North Sea

Bodo

Trondheim

Norway

Bergen

River Klarälven

Stavanger

Oslo

Sweden

Lake Vanern

Stockholm

Aland Islands

Göteborg

Lake Vattern

Jönköping

Gotland

Denmark

Oland

Copenhagen

Malmö

Bornholm

Baltic Sea

The Danish flag

The Norwegian flag

KM		250		500			1000	
MILES			250			500		

Herds of reindeer live in the forests of the far North.

In summer in the far North it never gets dark, even at night.

The forest trees are cut down and used to make houses, furniture and paper.

Logs are floated down rivers to sawmills.

The Finnish flag

The Swedish flag

Lapland

Lake Inari

Gulf of Bothnia

Finland

• Tampere

Helsinki

Seals live in the Gulf of Bothnia.

Finland has more than 50,000 lakes. Sweden has nearly 96,000 lakes!

Fact file

Highest mountain: Mount Glittertind, Norway, 2,472 m (8,110 ft).

Longest river: Glama River, Norway, 611 km (380 miles).

Weather: Scandinavia has long, cold, dark winters and short, mild summers.

Biggest city: Stockholm, Sweden, about 670,000 people.

Number of people: Finland, about 5 million. Norway, about 4 million. Sweden, about 8 million. Denmark, about 5 million.

| 1500 | | 2000 | | KM |
| | 1000 | | | MILES |

Britain and Central Europe

On this map you can see sixteen different countries. Some, like Luxembourg, are tiny. Others, such as France, are large. There are very high mountains, called the Alps, in Switzerland and Austria, but most of the rest of Europe is flatter. The flat land is very good for farming.

Britain used to be joined to the rest of Europe. It became an island a long time ago when sea levels rose.

Northern Ireland

Ireland is known as the Emerald Isle because of its beautiful green hills and fields.

The British Crown Jewels are kept safely locked in the Tower of London.

More than 300 different kinds of cheese are made in France.

Grapes are grown in parts of France and Germany. They are used to make wine.

The Eiffel Tower is in Paris, the capital of France.

Scotland
Glasgow
Edinburgh
Lough Neagh
Belfast
Great Britain
Newcastle
North Sea
Ireland
Dublin
Liverpool
Manchester
England
Wales
Birmingham
Cork
Cardiff
Bristol
London
Atlantic Ocean
English Channel

Denmark
Copenhagen
Hamburg
Berl
Amsterdam
Netherlands
Germany
Brussels
Cologne
Bonn
Belgium
Frankfurt
Luxembourg
River Rhine
Stuttgart
Le Havre
Rouen
River Seine
Paris
Strasbourg
Munich
Lake Constance
River Loire
Zürich
Bern
Switzerland
Lake Geneva
Geneva
Alps
Liechtenstein
France
Lyon
Bordeaux
River Rhône
Monaco
Toulouse
Marseille
Mediterranean Sea

	KM	250	500	1000	1500
	MILES		250	500	1000

The Netherlands are so flat that the sea can flood in. Sea walls protect the land and windmills pump water away. Many Dutch farmers grow flowers.

Germany, France and Britain have big factories making many things from cars to computers.

The Swiss flag

The British Union Jack

The French flag

The German flag

The Austrian flag

Gdansk

River Vistula

Warsaw

Poznan

Poland

River Oder

Wroclaw

River Elbe

Krakow

Carpathians

gue

Czechoslovakia

Vienna

Budapest

Hungary

Salzburg

Austria

River Danube

Cluj-Napoca

Romania

Constanta

Timisoara

Bucharest

Skiing is a popular sport in the mountains.

Bulgaria

Sofia

There are many fairytale castles built along the banks of the Rhine River in Germany.

Fact file

Highest mountain: Mont Blanc, France, 4,807 m (15,771 ft).

Longest river: The Danube, 2,824 km (1,755 miles).

Weather: Most of this part of Europe has mild winters and cool summers. Rain falls all year round. Snow falls on high land in winter.

Biggest city: Paris, France, about 10 million people.

Number of people in some European countries: France, about 56 million. Great Britain (England, Scotland and Wales), about 54 million. Germany, about 79 million. Netherlands, about 15 million. Luxembourg, about 380,000.

| 2000 | 2500 | 3000 | 3500 | KM |
| 1500 | | 2000 | | MILES |

Mediterranean Europe

The countries around the Mediterranean Sea are sunny all year. Olives, fruit and vegetables are grown in all these countries. Many people go to the Mediterranean for holidays. In parts of Spain and Italy there are high mountains where people ski in the winter.

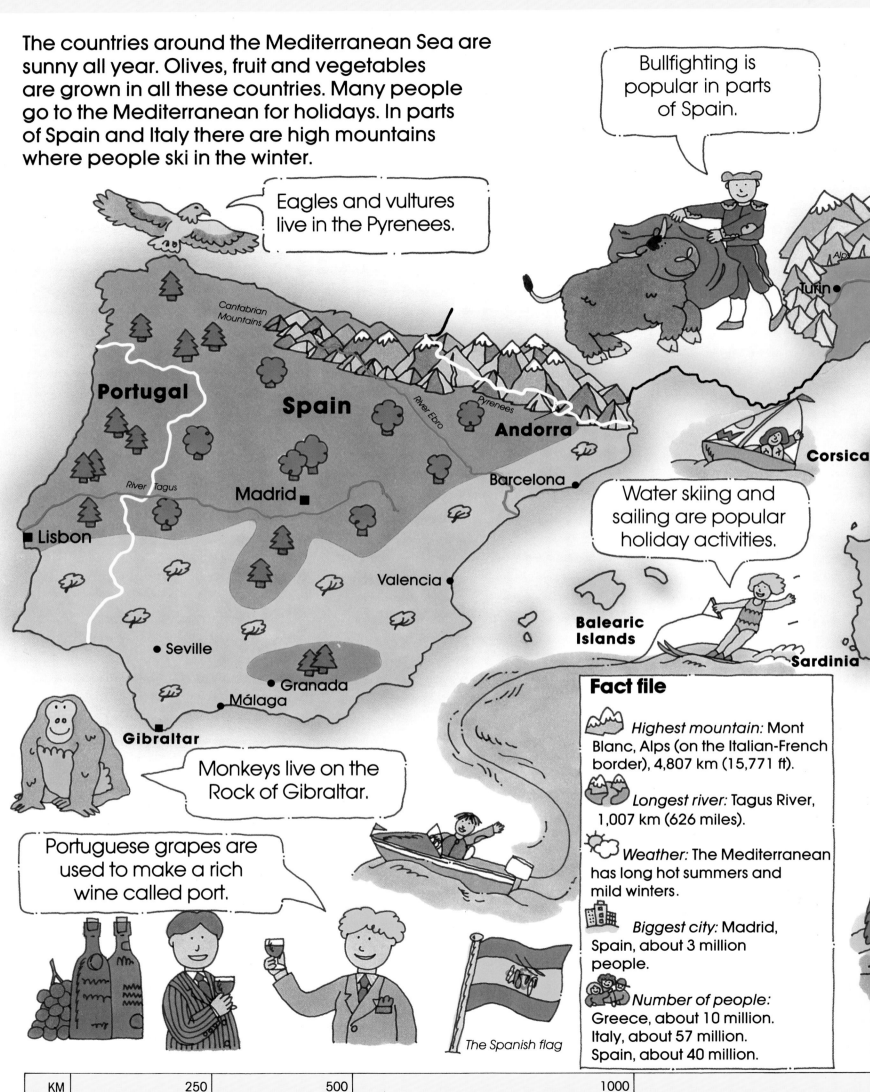

Bullfighting is popular in parts of Spain.

Eagles and vultures live in the Pyrenees.

Cantabrian Mountains

Portugal

Spain

River Ebro

Pyrenees

Andorra

Turin

Alps

Corsica

Barcelona

Water skiing and sailing are popular holiday activities.

River Tagus

Madrid

Lisbon

Valencia

Balearic Islands

Sardinia

Seville

Granada

Málaga

Gibraltar

Monkeys live on the Rock of Gibraltar.

Fact file

Highest mountain: Mont Blanc, Alps (on the Italian-French border), 4,807 km (15,771 ft).

Longest river: Tagus River, 1,007 km (626 miles).

Weather: The Mediterranean has long hot summers and mild winters.

Biggest city: Madrid, Spain, about 3 million people.

Number of people: Greece, about 10 million. Italy, about 57 million. Spain, about 40 million.

Portuguese grapes are used to make a rich wine called port.

The Spanish flag

KM		250		500			1000	
MILES			250			500		

Venice is built on many small islands in the sea. Many of the streets are canals, so people travel around the city in boats.

The herds of goats and sheep in the mountains provide milk, cheese, wool, butter and meat.

Dolomites

Slovenia

Ljubljana

Milan

Venice

Zagreb

River Po

Croatia

San Marino

Belgrade

Bosnia & Herzegovina

Florence

Pisa

Yugoslavia

Sarajevo

Serbia

Italy

Montenegro
Titograd

Turkey

Vatican City
Rome

Adriatic Sea

Skopje

Macedonia

Naples

Tiranë
Albania

Pindus Mountains

Most of Italy's factories are in the north of the country.

Greece

The Greek flag

Sicily

The Leaning Tower of Pisa in Italy has been leaning ever since it was built over 600 years ago.

Athens

There are over 1,400 Greek islands.

The Italian flag

Malta

Crete

Many people in southern Italy are farmers.

The Ancient Greeks and Romans built many fine temples and buildings. Today tourists go to see the ruins.

	2000		2500		KM
		1500			MILES

19

The Former U.S.S.R.

In 1991 the former U.S.S.R. (the Soviet Union) broke up into 15 separate republics. Estonia, Lithuania and Latvia became fully independent. Most of the other republics agreed to work together in a Commonwealth.

The north is freezing cold, but the deserts in the south are burning hot. In between there are forests and farmlands.

The Ural Mountains divide Europe from the Eastern part of Russia, which is in Asia.

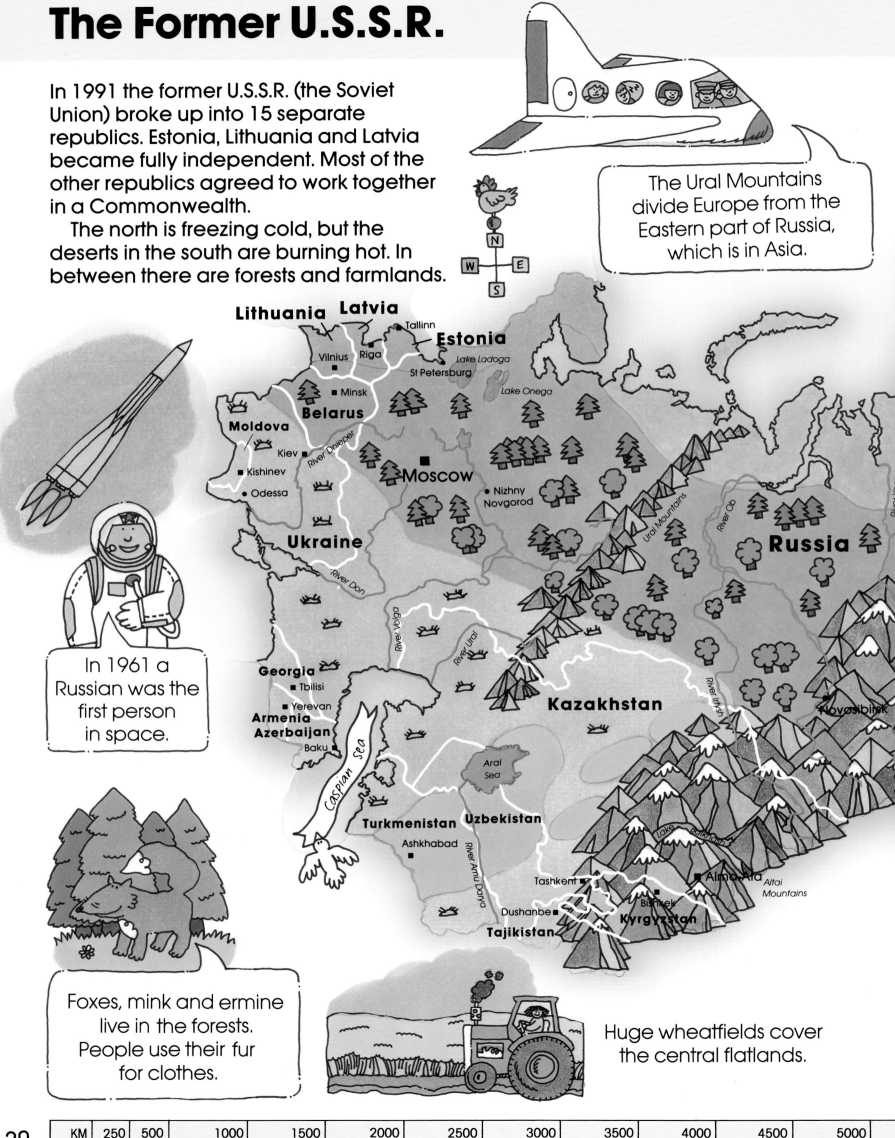

In 1961 a Russian was the first person in space.

Foxes, mink and ermine live in the forests. People use their fur for clothes.

Huge wheatfields cover the central flatlands.

Lithuania
Latvia
Tallinn
Estonia
Vilnius
Riga
Lake Ladoga
St Petersburg
Lake Onega
Minsk
Belarus
Moldova
Kiev
River Dnieper
Kishinev
Moscow
Odessa
Nizhny Novgorod
Ukraine
River Don
Ural Mountains
River Ob
River Yenisey
Russia
River Volga
River Ural
Georgia
Tbilisi
Yerevan
Armenia
Azerbaijan
Baku
Kazakhstan
River Irtysh
Novosibirsk
Caspian Sea
Aral Sea
Turkmenistan
Uzbekistan
Ashkhabad
River Amu Darya
Lake Balkhash
Tashkent
Alma-Ata
Altai Mountains
Bishkek
Dushanbe
Kyrgyzstan
Tajikistan

KM	250	500		1000	1500	2000	2500	3000	3500	4000	4500	5000
MILES		250	500		1000		1500		2000		2500		3000

Moscow, the capital of Russia, has beautiful old buildings with onion-shaped domes on top.

Arctic Ocean

Kolyma Mountains

Cherskiy Mountains

Verkhoyansk Mountains

River Lena

Sea of Okhotsk

River Amur

Lake Baikal

Vladivostok

Russian dancers, writers, and musicians, are known all over the world.

Many people spend their holidays by the Black Sea.

There are rich supplies of coal, oil and gas under the ground.

Fact file

Highest mountain: Communism Peak, 7495 m (24,590 ft).

Longest river: The Ob-Irtysh, 5,410 km (3,362 miles).

Largest city: Moscow, Russia, nearly 9 million.

Weather: In the north there is Arctic ice. In the south there is burning desert. Most places inland have hot summers and cold winters.

Number of people: About 280 million.

| 6000 | | 6500 | | 7000 | | 7500 | | 8000 | | 8500 | | 9000 | | 9500 | | 10,000 | | 10,500 | | KM |
| 4000 | | | 4500 | | | 5000 | | | 5500 | | | 6000 | | | 6500 | | MILES |

North America

North America contains Canada, the United States of America, Mexico, the countries of Central America and the West Indies. Canada is the second largest country in the world. The USA is the fourth largest and has fifty states.

The Canadian flag

Ice hockey is a very popular sport in Canada.

Skiing is popular in the Rocky mountains. The Rockies run from Canada, through the United States.

The USA produces more timber than any other country.

Canadian police are called Mounties. Some still ride horses, but most drive cars or motorcycles nowadays.

Alaska (USA)

Yukon River

Alaskan Mountains

Fairbanks •

• Anchorage

Great Bear Lake

Mackenzie River

Great Slave Lake

Lake Athabasca

Rocky Mountains

Vancouver •

Columbia River

Snake River

Coastal Mountains

Sierra Nevada

Colorado River

Los Angeles •
San Diego •

Fact file

 Highest mountain: Mount McKinley, Alaska, 6,194 km (20,322 ft).

Longest river: Mississippi River, USA, 3,779 km (2,384 miles).

Largest lake: Lake Superior, 82,103 sq km (31,700 sq miles).

Weather: Canada and Alaska are the coldest parts of North America. It is hot in central America and the West Indies.

Biggest city: New York, USA, about 7 million people.

Number of people: Canada, about 26 million. USA, about 249 million. Mexico, about 82 million. Costa Rica, about 3 million. Panama, about 2 million.

One of the world's most active volcanos, Mauna Loa, is on the island of Hawaii.

Hawaii (USA)

The Aztecs were a civilization in Mexico hundreds of years ago. Mexicans are proud of their Aztec ancestry.

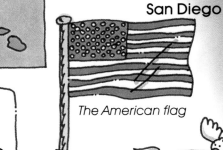
The American flag

Pacific Ocean

Bananas, coffee and sugar are grown in Central America.

The Mexican flag

KM	250	500	1000	1500	2000	2500	3000	3500	4000	4500	5000	5500	6000	6500
MILES		250	500	1000		1500	2000		2500		3000		3500	4000

Canadian Indians and Inuit were the first people to live in Canada.

Arctic Ocean

The Statue of Liberty was given to Americans by the French. It stands in New York harbour.

Atlantic Ocean

Beavers live in the forests and woods of Canada.

Canada

Lake Winnipeg
The Great Lakes
Lake Superior
Montreal
St Lawrence River
Ottawa ■
Toronto
Minneapolis
Lake Huron
Lake Michigan
Lake Ontario
Boston
Lake Erie
New York City
Chicago
Ohio River
Philadelphia

United States

Arkansas River
Mississippi River
Appalachian Mountains
Atlanta
Dallas
New Orleans
Rio Grande River
Houston
Miami

Gulf of Mexico

In the Caribbean Sea are thousands of islands called the West Indies, where it is sunny all year round.

Bermuda

The West Indies

The Bahamas
Cuba
Dominican Republic
Virgin Islands
Antigua & Barbuda
Guadeloupe
St Kitts – Nevis
Dominica
Puerto Rico
Barbados
Haiti
Martinique
St Lucia
Tobago
Jamaica
St Vincent
Grenada
Trinidad

The first rockets sent into space were launched from Cape Canaveral in Florida.

Mexico
Mexico City

Belize
Belmopan
Honduras
Guatemala
Guatemala City
Tegucigalpa
San Salvador
Nicaragua
El Salvador
Managua
San José
Panama City

Central America
Costa Rica
Panama

Hurricanes sometimes cause much damage in the West Indies.

Some American Indians carve totem poles out of wood.

	7500	8000	8500	9000	9500	10,000	10,500	11,000	11,500	12,000	12,500	13,000	13,500	KM
4500		5000		5500		6000		6500		7000		7500		8000	MILES

South America

South America is the fourth largest continent. It is made up of 13 different countries. There are mountains and rain forests as well as plains and deserts. The weather ranges from very hot to very cold.

The Brazilian flag

Hummingbirds are found in rain forests. They are very tiny and brightly coloured.

Anteaters also live in the rain forests. They use their long, sticky tongues to eat ants.

Rubber trees grow in South America. The tree bark is cut and the sticky sap runs out. It is collected to make rubber products.

Llamas are used to carry things in the Andes. Their thick fur protects them from the cold.

The Chilean flag

The Ecuadorean flag

Copper mines in northern Chile supply the world with copper.

Galapagos Islands

Ecuador

Caracas

Venezuela

Angel Falls

Guyana
Suriname
French
Guiana

Orinoco River

Georgetown

Guiana Highlands

Paramaribo

Cayenne

Bogotá

Colombia

Quito

Amazon River

Manaos

Lima

Peru

Bolivia

La Paz

Paraguay River

Brasilia

Chile

Paraguay

Asunción

Parana River

Andes Mountains

Santiago

Uruguay

Buenos Aires

Montevideo

Argentina

Falkland Islands

KM	250	500	1000	1500	2000	2500	3000	3500	4000	4500	5000	5500
MILES		250	500	1000		1500		2000		2500		3000	3500

The world's biggest bird, the condor, is found in South America. Its wings measure almost 3 metres (9 ft) across.

Patterns like these are woven into fabric by South American Indians.

Brazil

Atlantic Ocean

Brazilian Highlands

São Francisco River

Recife •

Salvador •

Rio de Janeiro •

The Incas built huge forts and temples about 500 years ago in the Andes mountains. The ruins of their buildings can still be seen.

The Bolivian flag

Fierce piranha fish live in the Amazon River.

Argentina has some of the largest cattle farms in the world. The cows are looked after by South American cowboys called gauchos.

Fact file

Highest mountains: Mount Aconcagua, Andes, Argentina, 6,959 m (22,831 ft).

Longest river: The Amazon is the second longest river in the world, 6,448 km (4,007 miles).

Largest lake: Lake Titicaca, Peru – Bolivia, 8,300 sq km (3,200 sq miles).

Highest waterfall: Angel falls in Venezuela is the highest in the world, 979 m (3,212 ft).

Biggest city: São Paulo, Brazil, about 10 million people.

Number of people in some countries: Chile, about 13 million. Argentina, about 32 million. Brazil, about 150 million.

The Colombian flag

The Peruvian flag

The Venezuelan flag

6500	7000	7500	8000	8500	9000	9500	10,000	10,500	11,000	11,500	KM
4000		4500		5000		5500	6000		6500	7000	MILES

Africa

Africa is the second largest continent in the world. It is split up into lots of different countries. Most of Africa is covered in grassland and desert. Some of the tropical rain forests in Africa have been chopped down to build villages and farms.

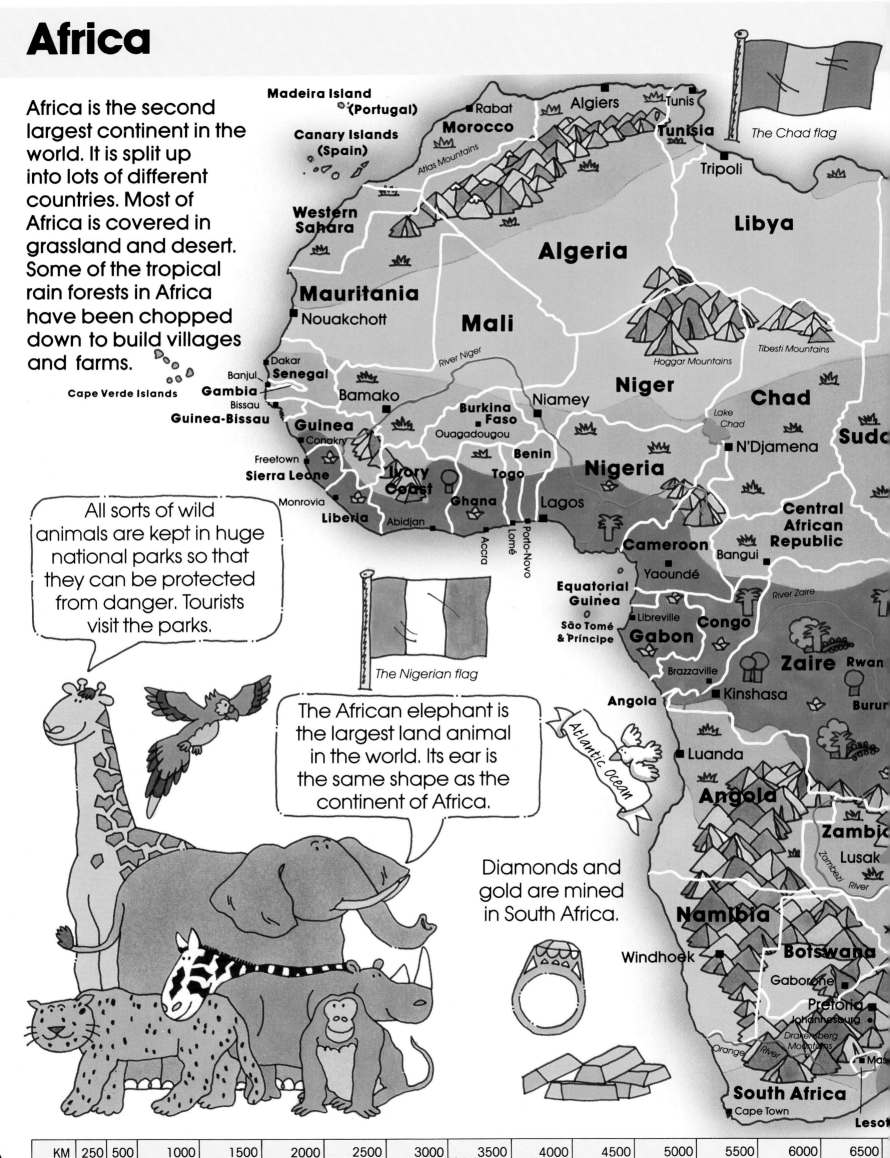

The Chad flag

Madeira Island (Portugal)

Canary Islands (Spain)

Cape Verde Islands

Rabat
Morocco
Algiers
Tunis
Tunisia
Tripoli
Libya

Atlas Mountains

Western Sahara

Algeria

Mauritania
Nouakchott

Mali

River Niger

Hoggar Mountains

Tibesti Mountains

Dakar
Senegal
Banjul
Gambia
Bissau
Guinea-Bissau
Guinea
Conakry

Bamako

Burkina Faso
Ouagadougou

Niamey

Niger

Chad

Lake Chad

N'Djamena

Sudu

Freetown
Sierra Leone
Monrovia
Liberia

Ivory Coast
Abidjan
Accra

Ghana
Lagos

Togo
Benin
Lomé
Porto-Novo

Nigeria

Central African Republic
Bangui

Cameroon
Yaoundé

Equatorial Guinea
São Tomé & Príncipe

Libreville
Gabon
Brazzaville

Congo

River Zaire

Zaire
Rwan

Kinshasa
Burur

Angola

Atlantic Ocean

Luanda

Angola

Zambi
Lusak

Zambezi River

Namibia

Windhoek

Botswana

Gaborone

Pretoria
Johannesburg

Drakensberg Mountains

Orange River

South Africa
Cape Town

Lesot

All sorts of wild animals are kept in huge national parks so that they can be protected from danger. Tourists visit the parks.

The Nigerian flag

The African elephant is the largest land animal in the world. Its ear is the same shape as the continent of Africa.

Diamonds and gold are mined in South Africa.

26

KM	250	500	1000	1500	2000	2500	3000	3500	4000	4500	5000	5500	6000	6500
MILES		250	500	1000		1500		2000		2500		3000		3500	4000

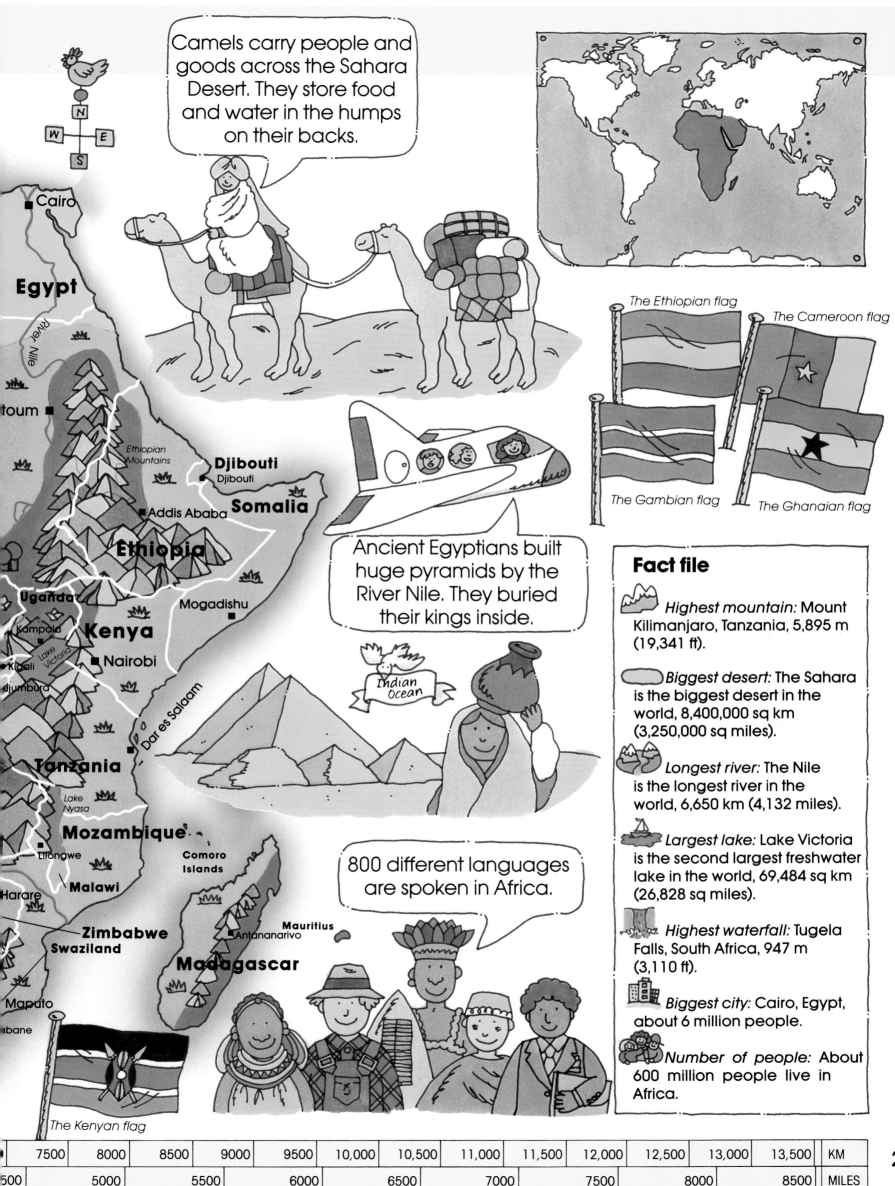

Camels carry people and goods across the Sahara Desert. They store food and water in the humps on their backs.

Ancient Egyptians built huge pyramids by the River Nile. They buried their kings inside.

800 different languages are spoken in Africa.

The Ethiopian flag

The Cameroon flag

The Gambian flag

The Ghanaian flag

The Kenyan flag

Cairo

Egypt

toum

River Nile

Ethiopian Mountains

Djibouti
Djibouti

Somalia

Addis Ababa

Ethiopia

Uganda

Kampala

Lake Victoria

Kigali

Njumbura

Kenya

Nairobi

Mogadishu

Dar es Salaam

Tanzania

Lake Nyasa

Mozambique

Lilongwe

Malawi

Harare

Zimbabwe

Swaziland

Maputo

bane

Comoro Islands

Mauritius
Antananarivo

Madagascar

Indian Ocean

Fact file

Highest mountain: Mount Kilimanjaro, Tanzania, 5,895 m (19,341 ft).

Biggest desert: The Sahara is the biggest desert in the world, 8,400,000 sq km (3,250,000 sq miles).

Longest river: The Nile is the longest river in the world, 6,650 km (4,132 miles).

Largest lake: Lake Victoria is the second largest freshwater lake in the world, 69,484 sq km (26,828 sq miles).

Highest waterfall: Tugela Falls, South Africa, 947 m (3,110 ft).

Biggest city: Cairo, Egypt, about 6 million people.

Number of people: About 600 million people live in Africa.

	7500	8000	8500	9000	9500	10,000	10,500	11,000	11,500	12,000	12,500	13,000	13,500	KM
500		5000		5500		6000		6500		7000		7500		8000	8500	MILES

The Middle East

Most of the Middle East is either mountainous or hot, sandy desert. Some of the countries have a great deal of valuable oil under the ground. The oil is pumped up to the surface at oil wells. It is then sold to other countries for use as petrol and other kinds of fuel.

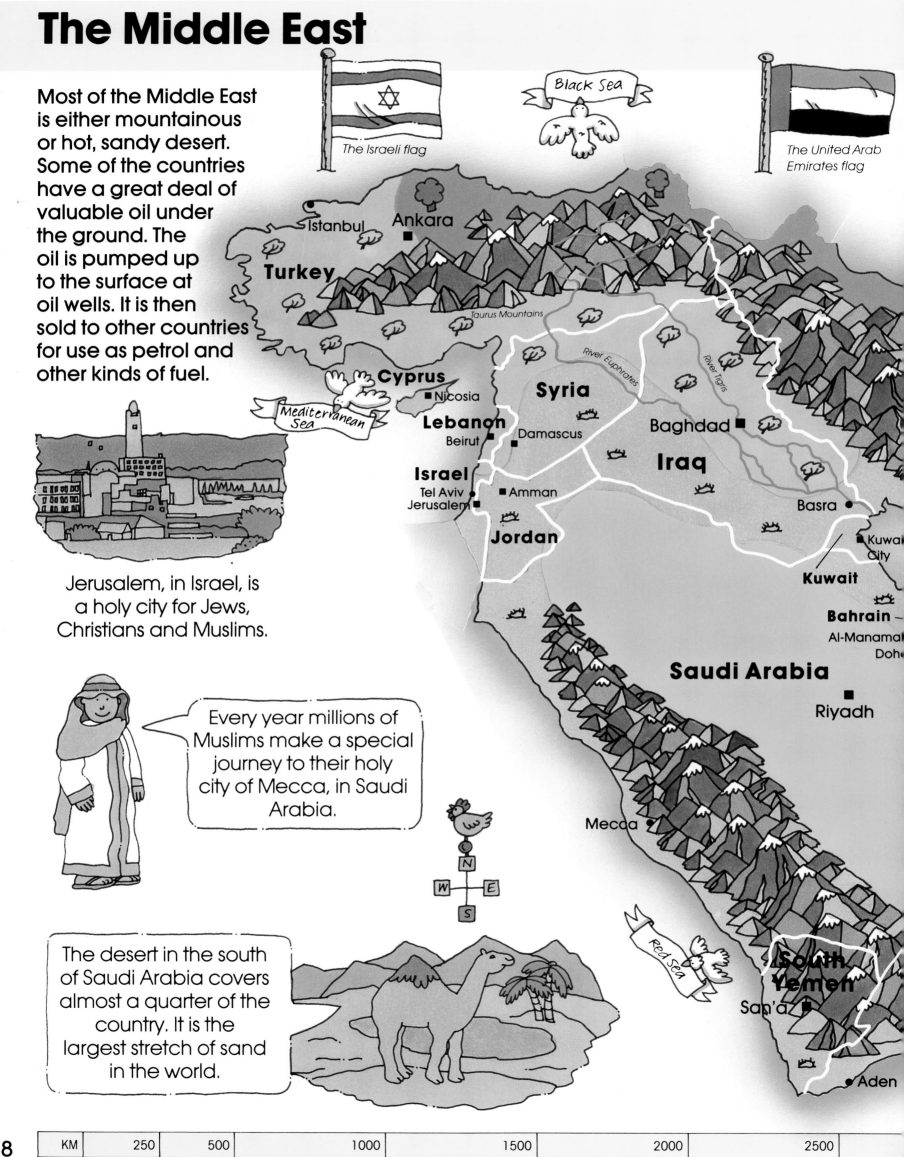

The Israeli flag

Black Sea

The United Arab Emirates flag

Jerusalem, in Israel, is a holy city for Jews, Christians and Muslims.

Every year millions of Muslims make a special journey to their holy city of Mecca, in Saudi Arabia.

The desert in the south of Saudi Arabia covers almost a quarter of the country. It is the largest stretch of sand in the world.

Istanbul
Ankara
Turkey
Taurus Mountains
Cyprus
Nicosia
Mediterranean Sea
Syria
River Euphrates
River Tigris
Lebanon
Beirut
Damascus
Baghdad
Iraq
Israel
Tel Aviv
Jerusalem
Amman
Basra
Jordan
Kuwait City
Kuwait
Bahrain
Al-Manama
Doha
Saudi Arabia
Riyadh
Mecca
N
W
E
S
Red Sea
South Yemen
San'a
Aden

KM	250	500	1000	1500	2000	2500
MILES	250	500	1000	1500		

Leopards live in the mountains of Iran.

Afghanistan

■ Kabul

Hindu Kush

Elburz Mountains

Tehran

Iran

Zagros Mountains

Persian Gulf

Qatar

■ Abu Dhabi

United Arab Emirates

Oman

Muscat ■

Oman

Yemen

The Saudi Arabian flag

Oil is carried by pipe line from oil wells to ports. Ships take the oil all over the world.

The Iranian flag

There is very little rain in these countries. Some water is found in deep underground wells. Seawater can also be purified for drinking.

Nomadic tribes live in parts of Iran. They live in tents, travelling from place to place with their goats and sheep.

Beautiful rugs and carpets are made in Iran.

Fact file

Highest mountains: Elburz Mountains, Iran, over 5,600 m (18,300 ft).

Longest river: The Euphrates, 2,740 km (1,703 miles).

Weather: These countries have very hot summers and cool winters.

Biggest city: Tehran, Iran, about 6 million people.

Number of people: Israel, about 4.7 million. Iran, about 56 million. Iraq, about 18 million. Saudi Arabia, about 14 million.

| 3000 | 3500 | 4000 | 4500 | 5000 | 5500 | KM |
| 2000 | | 2500 | | 3000 | 3500 | MILES |

South Asia

Much of South Asia is farmland, and relies on the heavy monsoon rains between June and October for crops to grow. The Himalayas are the highest mountain range in the world and divide South Asia from China.

The Himalayas are too icy to cross in winter.

Crops need the monsoon rains, but the storms sometimes cause terrible floods, which can destroy whole villages.

The shape of the Indian elephant's ear is the same as the outline of India.

Many people in South Asia eat rice every day.

More tea is grown in India than anywhere else in the world.

Islamabad

Lahore

Delhi
New Delhi

Nepal
Kathmandu

Pakistan

River Indus

Thar desert

Kanpur · River Ganges

Ahmadabad

India

Bombay

Hyderabad

Bay of Bengal

Cal

The Pakistani flag

Bangalore

Madras

The Sri Lankan flag

Colombo

Sri Lanka

The Indian flag

Him

KM	250	500		1000	1500		2000		2500
MILES		250	500			1000			1500

Ponies, yaks and even sheep are used to carry goods across the Himalayas.

Bhutan
Thimbu
River Brahmaputra
Bangladesh
Dhaka

Elephants and tigers live on the lower slopes of the Himalayas and in the swamps of the Ganges River.

India is the second most crowded country in the world.

Fact file

Highest mountain: Mount Everest, Himalayas, 8,848 m (29,029 ft).

Longest river: Ganges-Brahmaputra, 2,900 km (1,802 miles).

Weather: It is very cold in the mountains, but hot most of the year elsewhere.

Biggest city: Calcutta, India, about 9 million people.

Number of people in some countries:
Nepal, about 18 million.
Bangladesh, about 110 million.
Bhutan, about 1.5 million.
India, about 850 million.
Sri Lanka, about 17 million.
Pakistan, about 120 million.

Cows are sacred animals in India. They are not kept in fields but are allowed to graze where they like.

Cotton plants produce threads that are made into cotton fabric. It can be painted or dyed and made into clothes.

The Taj Mahal, near Agra in northern India, is often called the most beautiful building in the world.

| 3000 | | 3500 | | 4000 | | 4500 | | 5000 | | KM |
| | 2000 | | | 2500 | | | 3000 | | | MILES |

Southeast Asia and Pacific Islands

Southeast Asia and the Pacific Islands is an area that curves from Myanmar through a chain of islands towards Australia. It is warm all the year round, but the monsoon wind brings heavy rains. They can damage the traditional houses made of woven palm leaves.

In Thailand, elephants are used to haul trees from the forest to the river. The trees then float down to the sawmills.

Coral are sea creatures that live in the warm, shallow waters of the Pacific. When they die, their hard skeletons form islands and reefs. Millions of coral are needed to make one small island.

Fishing is a way of life for many islanders. Their boats are like canoes with small sails.

Coral islands when seen from above have a turquoise band of sea around them.

The Thai flag

Mandalay

Myanmar

Yangon

Thailand

Bangkok

Laos

Vientiane

Hanoi

Vietnam

Cambodia

Phnom Penh

South China Sea

Ho Chi Minh City

Brunei

Bandar Seri Begawan

Medan

Kuala Lumpur

Malaysia

Singapore

Jakarta

Indonesia

Semarang

Surabaya

Bandung

Irrawaddy River

KM	250	500	1000	1500	2000	2500	3000	35
MILES		250	500	1000	1500		2000	

There are a few factories around Manila, but most people live by growing rice and catching fish.

Many of the mountains are volcanoes.

The Philippines are made up of over 7,000 islands.

A volcano is a hole where molten rock gushes out from under the Earth. So much comes out that new mountains are formed around the hole.

Philippines

Manila

Cebu •

The Singaporean flag

Fact file

Highest mountain: Puncak Jaya, New Guinea, 5,030 m (16,503 ft).

Longest river: Mekong River, Cambodia, 4,350 km (2,703 miles).

Weather: It is warm all year round, with cooling sea breezes. The monsoon wind brings heavy rainfall, and sometimes there are strong winds called typhoons.

Biggest city: Jakarta, Indonesia, about 9 million.

Number of people in some countries: Philippines, about 60 million. Thailand, about 55 million. Malaysia, about 18 million. Indonesia, about 180 million.

Some of the animals in New Guinea are like those in nearby Australia, such as the wallaby.

Indonesia

Papua New Guinea

The Papua New Guinean flag

Port Moresby ■

| | 4000 | | 4500 | | 5000 | | 5500 | | 6000 | | 6500 | | 7000 | KM |
| 2500 | | | 3000 | | | 3500 | | | 4000 | | | | MILES |

East Asia

China is the third largest country in the world. Japan is much smaller, about the same size as Britain, but it is the richest country in Asia.

Chinese temples and pagodas have tiled roofs that curl up at the corners.

W N E S

The Mongolian flag

Ulan Bator

Altai Mountains

Mongolia

Gobi Desert

China

Huang He

Tibetan Plateau

Taiyuan

Himalayas

Tibet

Xian

River Mekong

Chengdu

Chang Jiang

Guangzhou

The Chinese flag

Fact file

Highest mountain: Mount Everest, 8,848 m (29,029 ft).

Longest river: Chang Jiang, China, 5,530 km (3,436 miles).

Weather: Northern China and Japan have wet summers and dry winters. The south is very hot all year round.

Biggest city: Tokyo, Japan, about 8 million people.

Number of people: Japan, about 123 million. China, about 1.1 billion.

KM	250	500	1000	1500	2000	2500	3000
MILES		250	500	1000		1500	

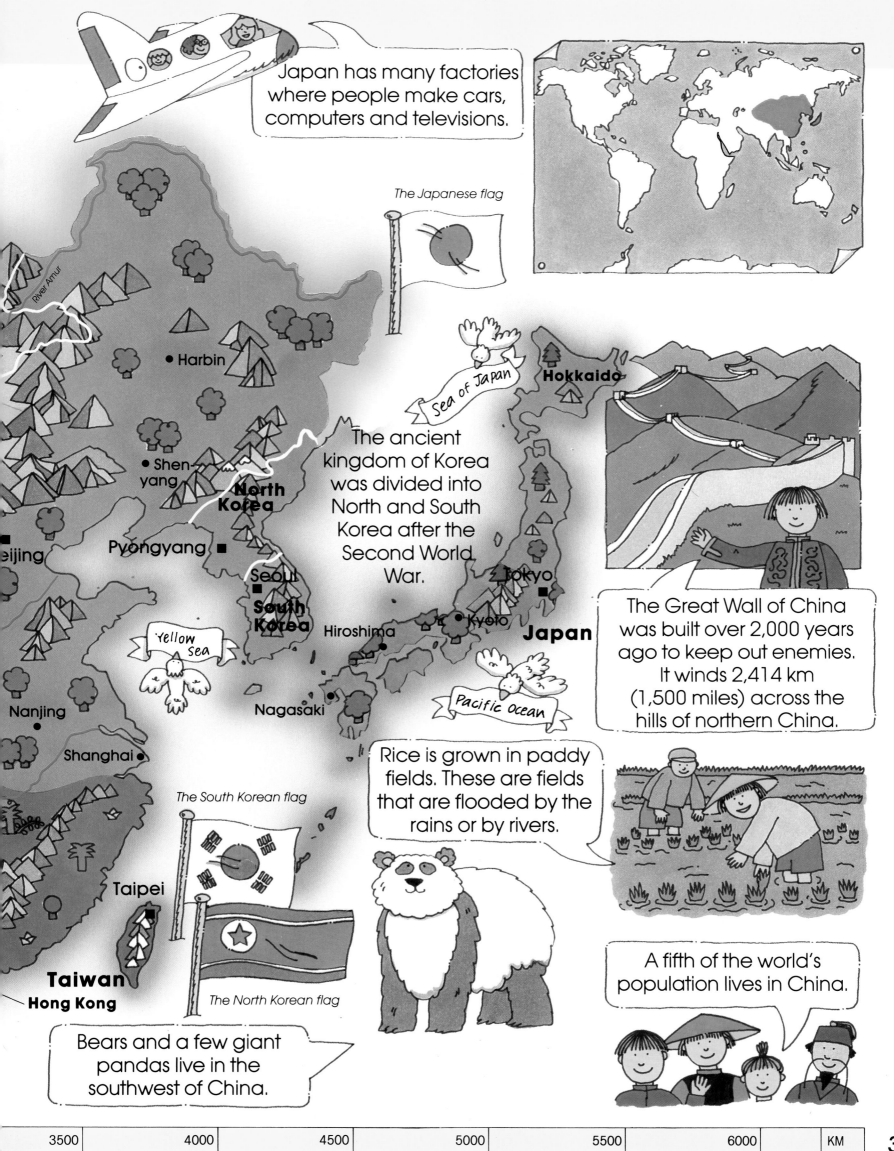

Japan has many factories where people make cars, computers and televisions.

The Japanese flag

The ancient kingdom of Korea was divided into North and South Korea after the Second World War.

Sea of Japan

Hokkaido

The Great Wall of China was built over 2,000 years ago to keep out enemies. It winds 2,414 km (1,500 miles) across the hills of northern China.

River Amur

Harbin

Shen-yang

North Korea

Pyongyang

eijing

Seoul

South Korea

Hiroshima

Yellow Sea

Nanjing

Nagasaki

Tokyo

Kyoto

Japan

Pacific Ocean

Shanghai

The South Korean flag

Rice is grown in paddy fields. These are fields that are flooded by the rains or by rivers.

Taipei

Taiwan

Hong Kong

The North Korean flag

A fifth of the world's population lives in China.

Bears and a few giant pandas live in the southwest of China.

| 3500 | 4000 | 4500 | 5000 | 5500 | 6000 | KM |
| | 2500 | | 3000 | | 3500 | MILES |

Australia and New Zealand

Australia is the smallest continent in the world. It lies in the southern Pacific Ocean, on the opposite side of the world from Europe. New Zealand is 1,500 km (900 miles) southeast of Australia. Most of Australia is flat and dry. New Zealand is more hilly and green.

Australia is nearly 59 times bigger than England.

There are huge sheep farms in Australia. The country produces the largest amount of wool in the world.

Fact file

Highest mountain: Mount Cook, New Zealand, 3,764 m (12,349 ft).

Longest river: River Darling, Australia, 2,739 km (1,702 miles).

Weather: Parts of Australia are very hot desert. New Zealand is cooler and has more rain.

Biggest city: Sydney, Australia, about 3.5 million people.

Number of people: Australia, about 17 million. New Zealand, about 3 million.

Timor Sea

Darwin

Hamersley Range

Alice Springs

Macdonnell Ranges

Australia

Great Victoria Desert

Perth

Kangaroos, koalas and wombats all have pouches for their young.

Koalas live in trees and eat eucalyptus leaves.

The duck-billed platypus is a rare animal found only in Australia.

| KM | | 250 | 500 | | 1000 | | 1500 | | 2000 | | 2500 | |
| MILES | | | 250 | | 500 | | | 1000 | | | 1500 | |

The Arctic

The Arctic is the area around the North Pole. It is frozen ocean surrounded by land. The ocean is covered with ice that slowly drifts from place to place.

The Icelandic flag

Polar bears live on the frozen sea. They catch seals to eat.

Alaska

Arctic Ocean

North Pole

Russia

Canada

Arctic Ocean

Greenland

Godthab

Iceland

Reykjavik

Arctic Circle

Sweden

Finland

Norway

Inuit people live in the Arctic parts of Canada, Alaska and Greenland.

In summer, most of the Arctic land is covered with plants. Grass and mosses grow there and many flowers bloom.

KM	250	500	1000	1500	2000	2500	3000	3500	4000	4500	KM
MILES		250	500	1000		1500		2000		2500		MILES

The Antarctic

The Antarctic is ice-covered land around the South Pole. The ice is 4,500 metres (14,800 feet) thick in some places. There are many high mountains and some volcanoes.

At the North and South Poles, winter and summer last six months each. Winter is dark all day and night. In summer it is light all the time.

The Arctic

The Antarctic

When it is winter at one Pole, it is summer at the other.

Atlantic Ocean

Antarctic Peninsula

South Pole

Antarctic

Amery ice shelf

Transantarctic Mountains

Ross ice shelf

Pacific Ocean

Antarctic Circle

The Antarctic is the coldest place on Earth. The only people living there are scientists.

Whales, fish, birds and seals live around the coast, but there are no plants or land animals.

Penguins are Antarctic birds. They cannot fly but they swim very well.

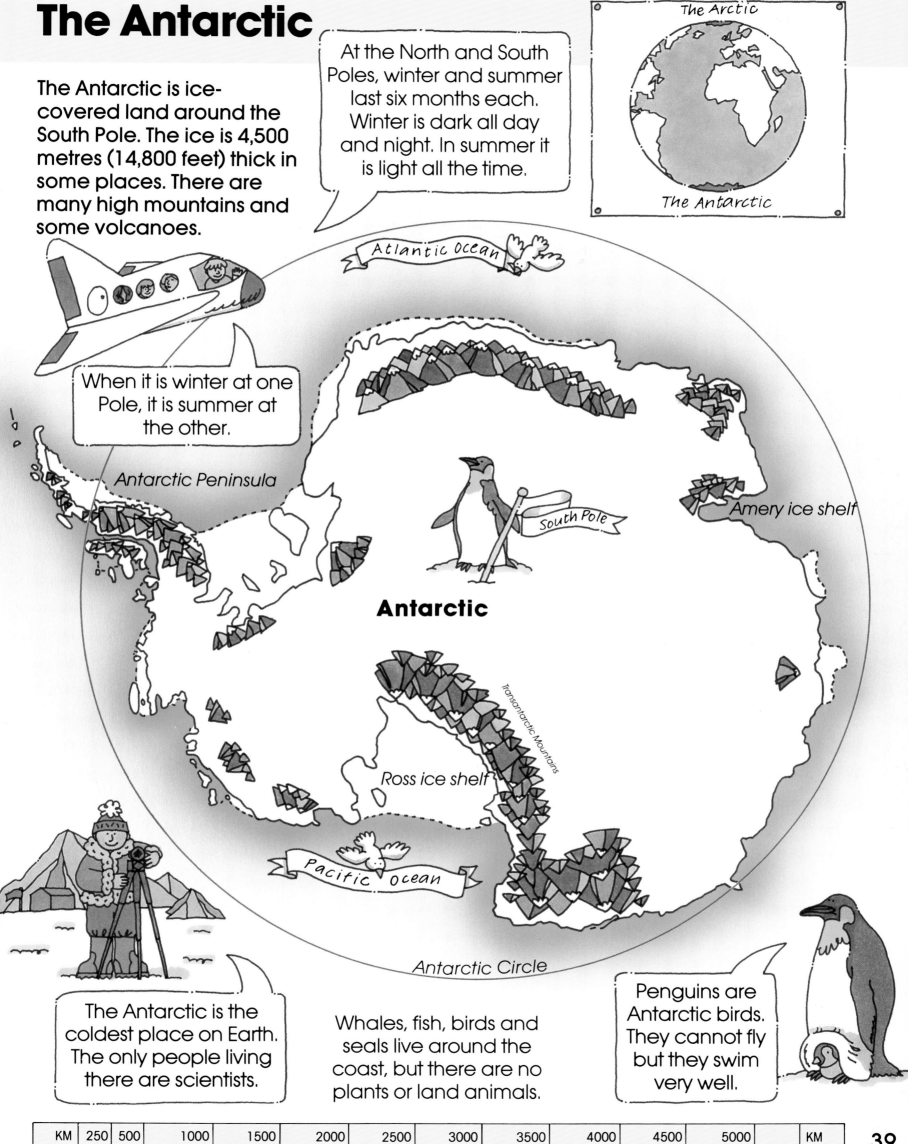

KM	250	500	1000	1500	2000	2500	3000	3500	4000	4500	5000	KM
MILES		250	500	1000		1500		2000		2500		3000	MILES

39

Index

This book was created and produced by Times Four Publishing Ltd., High Street, Cuckfield, Sussex RH17 5EN.

Copyright ©1991 Times Four Publishing Ltd.

All rights reserved. No part of this book may be reproduced or transmitted in any form or by any means, electronic or mechanical, including photocopying, recording, or by any information storage and retrieval system, without permission in writing from the publisher.

Map consultants: Sussex University Map Library
Geography consultants: Diane Snowdon, Keith Lye

Typeset by Amber Graphics, Burgess Hill, Sussex.
Colour separations by RCS Graphics Ltd., Leeds.
Printed by Proost, Belgium

First published in the UK in 1992 by The Watts Group

BRITISH LIBRARY CATALOGUING IN PUBLICATION DATA
A catalogue record for this book is available from the British Library.

ISBN 0 7496 0829 3 HB

ISBN 0 7496 30000 PB

10   9   8   7   6   5   4   3   2   1